THE AZTECS

THE

AZTECS

BY BARBARA L. BECK
Revised by
LORNA GREENBERG

A GROLIER COMPANY

A First Book/Revised Edition
FRANKLIN WATTS
New York/London/Toronto/Sydney/1983

Diagrams and map courtesy of
Vantage Art, Inc.

Cover illustration: A two-headed serpent,
fashioned of jade and shells.
Courtesy of the British Museum.

Interior photographs courtesy of
The Metropolitan Museum of Art: frontis, p. 14;
Walter R. Aguiar: p. 3;
American Museum of Natural History:
pp. 4, 12, 22, 26, 31, 36, 41, 49, 54, 55;
Mexican Government Tourism Office: pp. 7, 20, 33, 46;
The Museum of Primitive Art: p. 58.

Library of Congress Cataloging in Publication Data

Beck, Barbara L.
The Aztecs.

(A First book)
Rev. ed. of: The first book of the Aztecs. 1966.
Bibliography: p.
Includes index.
Summary: Discusses the beginnings of the ancient
American civilization, its people and their way
of life, and the coming of the Spanish conquistadores.
1. Aztecs—Juvenile literature. I. Aztecs.
2. Indians of Mexico I. Greenberg, Lorna. II. Beck,
Barbara L. First book of the Aztecs. III. Title.
F1219.73.B4   1983   972'.01   82-16013
ISBN 0-531-04522-6

CONTENTS

THE AZTECS

THE AZTECS

Chapultepec •

Gulf of Mexico

Ila Venta •

San Lorenzo •
★ Tenochtitlán

Tres Zapotes •

Veracruz •

Tlacopan •

Teotihuacan •
Tula • Texcoco •
Santa Cecilia ★ • Tlaxcala
Tenayuca ★ Coyoacán • Cholula
Xochimilco •

Culhuacán •

Monte Albán ★ • Oaxaca

V   A   L   L   E   Y   O   F   M   E   X   I   C   O

HONDURAS

EL SALVADOR

NICARAGUA

GUATEMALA

Pacific Ocean

——— Aztec realm
– – – Maya realm
• Aztec cities
★ Archeological sites

1

FINDING A HOME
IN THE NEW WORLD

About twenty thousand years ago, or earlier, we believe that people came to the Americas from the continent of Asia. They reached the New World by way of the Bering Strait land bridge—a chain of islands and land masses that formed a passage between Asia and North America. The land bridge is now covered by the water of the North Pacific Ocean. But for thousands of years small bands of primitive peoples used it, to cross back and forth, searching for better food-gathering, hunting, and fishing grounds. Gradually they moved further into North America, to the south and east, following the herds of wild animals. These people were the ancestors of the earliest American Indians.

By 11,000 B.C., these hunting peoples had spread through nearly all of the New World. They fished in the lakes, hunted down the ancient elephants called mastodons, killed mammoths, bison, bears, and smaller game. They gathered wild grasses, berries, grains, nuts, and sunflower seeds for food. Their tools were made of stone or bone, and their clothing of animal skins. Their shelters were often caves.

Many more years passed before some of these people found, perhaps by accident, that plants could grow from seeds poked into the ground. Planting seeds and cultivating and harvesting plants brought a new way of life. Now they could settle in one place, build permanent shelters, make better tools and clothing, and learn better ways to cook. Not all American Indians turned to farming; some continued living as hunters and food gatherers.

We are not sure when the early people reached the fertile area called the Valley of Mexico. But by 6500 B.C., there were farming families living there, growing chili peppers, cotton, and squash. Between 5000 and 3500 B.C., they began to grow Indian corn, or maize. Maize became the basic food of all the people in the Valley.

The Valley of Mexico lies about 7,000 feet (2,100 m) above sea level. It is ringed by mountains, many of them volcanic. In early times there were many lakes, surrounded by fertile soil. Very gradually, the early farmers settled in here. They formed communities which then, slowly, worked out separate ways of living. The communities had many ties—they shared their dependence on maize and farmed it in the same way, and they shared their worship of nature. But they developed different languages, different styles in building and in their crafts, and different customs and styles of clothing.

Scholars now believe the Olmec may have been the earliest civilization to develop in Mexico and Central America. From about 1200 to 300 B.C., the Olmec people built cities, or centers, at La Venta, Tres Zapotes, and San Lorenzo on the southern Gulf Coast. Here, in thick green jungles swarming with insects and deadly snakes and animals, archeologists have found the Olmecs' ruined pyramids, plazas, and giant stone heads, as high as 8 feet (2. m) and weighing up to 20 tons.

The Olmecs created colossal, mysterious stone heads like this one near San Lorenzo.

The vast Zapotec site of Monte Albán
includes temples, pyramids, a ball court, tombs,
underground passages, and huge plazas.

These heads all have thick-lipped, babylike faces, in a style we call Olmec.

The Olmecs developed a system of counting, and a system of picture writing in which pictures or symbols called hieroglyphs (glyphs) stand for words. They could also measure the passing of time. They put up large slabs of stone, called *stelae*, on which they carved hieroglyphic figures. Some figures record important dates in their history. Many scholars feel that the Olmec people of La Venta developed these sciences and skills first and that later Central American civilizations borrowed or copied from them.

From the time of the Olmecs, other peoples formed civilizations. To the southwest lived a people called the Zapotecs (ZAH-po-teks). Their main ceremonial city was Monte Albán. It was built on the top of a small mountain that had been leveled to make a platform for the city's great temples. North of the Zapotecs lived the Mixtecs (MEE-steks), who developed fine skills at goldworking and made beautiful painted books called codices, which, in picture writing, told their history.

Between the first and seventh centuries, a strong northern tribe built a magnificent city called Teotihuacan (tay-o-TEE-wah-kahn). This city, which spread over an area of about 8 square miles (20.8 sq km), was ancient Mexico's greatest. The population may have been over 150,000. The powerful Teotihuacan civilization lasted for about seven hundred years and its influence was spread as far as Guatemala.

The Teotihuacan culture collapsed about the end of the seventh century, during a time of unrest. While we are not sure of the reasons, many of the civilizations in the Valley had been weakened by revolt, famine, and religious problems. At this time, too, waves of rough, unsettled people — barbarians — flooded in from the north.

While Teotihuacan flourished in the Valley, another culture — the Maya — reached its height in lands further to the south. This civilization, too, mysteriously crumbled after A.D. 900. Its people scattered through the region, and its power was lost.

In the ninth century a wandering people, the Toltecs, moved into the Valley and founded a city we call Tula. The Toltecs were skilled in politics and in military organization. They built an empire, ruling over many other groups and tribes of north and central Mexico. They were unequaled in their crafts and were clever artists. The Toltecs, and later the Aztecs, spoke a language called Nahuatl (NAH-wahtl).

When the Toltec empire fell apart, about 1200, its people spread through Mexico, taking their skills and culture with them. With the Toltec empire gone, many states and peoples struggled for power. Tula was taken over by a group of Chichimecs (CHEE-chee-meks)—a name given to the tribes of rough nomadic hunter-gatherers, or barbarians, who roamed through the dry plateau regions. These Chichimecs, or "Dog People," were said to eat raw meat and wear animal skins.

Among the groups competing for land and power were a people called the Tenochca, or Mexica. These are the people we now call the Aztecs. The Aztecs were the last tribe of barbarians to arrive in the Valley of Mexico. They came down from the north in the thirteenth century. Then, in just over three hundred years—from about 1215 to 1521, when they were conquered by the Spanish—they built a vast and powerful nation. At their peak, the Aztecs controlled 80,000 square miles (208,000 sq km) of land; they had conquered between four hundred and five hundred different states and ruled twelve to fifteen million people.

The history of the Aztec civilization has been pieced together from a variety of sources. From Aztec painters and scribes, we have the detail-filled picture books called codices. There are reports from the Spanish conquistadores and from the missionaries, officials, and priests who came after them. Finally, we have information from archeologists and other scientists who have explored and studied the remains of the Aztec past.

Only a few of the Aztec codices from before the Conquest still exist. The Spanish destroyed most, because they thought these books were filled with magic and evil. But a dozen or so had been sent home by the Spanish, perhaps as curiosities. These are now in libraries in Europe.

Teotihuacan was the first true city in central
Mexico. Through the heart of the city ran a
wide avenue, lined by pyramids, temples, and plazas
that led to the Great Pyramid of the Sun.

After the Conquest, the Indians learned the alphabet writing system of the Spanish. They used Spanish letters then to write in their own language, Nahuatl, or in Spanish. Three important books from this time are the *Codex Mendoza* and the *Codex Florentino*, which both describe Aztec life and customs, and the *Codex Magliabecchiano, The Book of Life of the Ancient Mexicans*. These and other codices are filled with history, ritual, prophecy, astronomy, songs, speeches, and general lore.

Among the most important writings of the Spanish invaders are five letters from Hernán Cortés, leader of the conquistadores, to his king, Emperor Charles V of Spain. One of Cortés's soldiers, Bernal Díaz del Castillo, wrote *The True History of the Conquest of New Spain* when he was eighty-four. It describes bloody battles, endless marches, days without food and water, and the final siege and fall of the great Aztec capital, Tenochtitlán (tay-noch-tee-TLAHN).

In 1529, eight years after the Conquest, Father Bernardino de Sahagún came to Mexico. With the help of the Aztecs he wrote, in Nahuatl, *General History of the Affairs of New Spain*. Today Sahagún's reports of Indian life are of priceless value to historians.

There are hundreds of accounts of life in Mexico both before and soon after the Conquest. Many later scholars have based their writings on these accounts and on the findings of the archeologists. There are over five thousand important archeological sites in Mexico. Some have scarcely been touched, while at others magnificent temples, broad roads, sculptures, paintings, and the tools of daily living have been found. They give us a realistic and exciting picture of the Aztecs and their way of life.

2

THE BEGINNING OF
THE AZTEC NATION

The barbarian people who were to become the Aztecs left their legendary home, Aztlan (or Aztatlan), "Place of the Herons," in the north of Mexico in 1168. Some Aztec records tell us the tribe first lived on an island in a lake. One day they found in a nearby cave an idol who spoke to them. The idol was called Huitzilopochtli (wee-tseel-o-POTCH-tlee), "Hummingbird Wizard" or "Blue Hummingbird." Huitzilopochtli ordered the Aztecs to leave their home and search for a new land.

After many years of wandering, carrying the idol with them, the Aztecs moved into the forest of Chapultepec (cha-pool-tuh-PEK), the "Hill of the Grasshopper," in the Valley of Mexico. Here they were scorned as rough, uncivilized people by the other groups already settled in the region. When they began to raid neighboring tribes for wives, war broke out. The Tepanec (tay-pah-NEK), Culhua, and Xochimilca (ho-chee-MEEL-kah) tribes attacked the Aztecs, forcing many to flee and taking others as slaves. The Aztecs became the subjects of the Culhuas.

In time the Culhuas and the Xochimilcas began to war between themselves. The Aztecs fought for their rulers, the Culhuas. After winning the battle, the Culhuan chief rewarded the Aztecs by giving his daughter to their chief. Following their customs, the Aztecs sacrificed her to Huitzilopochtli. They believed this was the greatest honor they could pay her. When the Culhuan chief arrived to attend his daughter's wedding and discovered what had happened, he set his warriors against the Aztecs. Many were killed; those who escaped fled to a swampy, snake-filled island in Lake Texcoco (tess-KO-ko), the "Lake of the Moon."

Some of the Aztec codices and records say that when Huitzilopochtli first told his people to seek a new land, he said they would know the right place when they saw an eagle eating a serpent while perched on a cactus with red, heart-shaped fruits. When the Aztecs arrived on the island in Lake Texcoco and saw this eagle, they knew they had found their home. The same symbol of the eagle appears on the flag of the Republic of Mexico today.

At first the Aztecs lived in miserable mud-and-reed huts. They were able to find food, for fish were plentiful in the lake, and the swamps were filled with birds, frogs, and snakes. Since there was almost no wood or stone on the island, the Aztecs bartered with the mainlanders for materials with which to build their town. The first building, a stone temple, was raised in 1325 in honor of their god, Huitzilopochtli.

The Aztecs were hated by their neighbors on the mainland, but they soon learned to provide for themselves. They built canals, bridges, and causeways or roads over the marshes that led to nearby islands. They made rafts of reeds, which they covered with mud and then anchored in the marshes or along the edges of nearby islands. The mud rafts were planted with vegetables. These floating gardens, called *chinampas* (chee-NAM-pahs), increased the amount of gardening land. The lake-bottom mud used in *chinampa* farming produced rich crops. *Chinampas* can still be seen today, south of Mexico City at a place called the Floating Gardens of Xochimilco.

Gradually the Aztecs turned their swampy island into a place of plenty. When more room for living was needed, the *chinampa* garden

[10]

areas were filled in and the space was used for new houses. The people called their city Tenochtitlán, "Place of the Prickly Pear Cactus."

At about this time one group of Aztecs broke away from the others and started building a twin city on a small nearby island. They called it Tlatelolco (tla-tel-OL-ko). The two cities were rivals for many years, partly because Tlatelolco had a bigger marketplace and the people of Tenochtitlán were jealous. Eventually Tlatelolco was conquered, the water between the cities was filled in, and Tlatelolco became a part of Tenochtitlán.

The early history of the Aztecs is filled with struggles and battles, alliances, or agreements, and broken alliances, and competition with neighboring tribes for land, water, and power. Through these years the Aztecs grew stronger; they became skilled at gaining and keeping power and building an empire. They learned from the cultures of the other peoples of the Valley, especially the scattered descendents of the great Toltecs. In fact they began to claim that the Toltecs were their own ancestors.

In 1375 Acamapichtli became the first king of the Aztec state. The Nahuatl title he took, *tlatoani*, means "speaker" of the Aztecs. Later, after the state grew, the ruler was called *ueitlatoani*, "great speaker," to show he spoke not only for the Aztecs but also for all their subject tribes.

In 1427 the strong Itzcóatl (eets-KO-atl) became the fourth Aztec ruler. With his chief advisor, Tlacaélel — who was to serve Itzcóatl and the two kings who followed him — they reshaped the Aztec world. They fought and defeated the Tepanecs, freeing the Aztecs from their control. They took over dozens of other small city-states in the Valley and thus became the greatest state in Mexico. They entered into an alliance with the states of Texcoco and Tlacopán.

Itzcóatl and Tlacaélel then began the task of changing past history, so that the Aztecs' barbarian beginnings would be forgotten. They had all codices and records of the Aztecs burned. They then ordered the past rewritten, to show the Aztecs were the true descendants of the Toltecs and thus worthy to rule Mexico. They were also the people chosen to keep the sun moving across the sky.

In 1440 Itzcóatl died and another remarkable king came to power. He was Montezuma I, who was also known as Ilhuicamina (ell-wee-kah-MEEN-ah), the "Wrathful." His name was Mohtecuzomatzin; but in English it is often simplified to Montezuma, or Moctezuma, or Motecuhzuma. He led his warriors to victory over many tribes and stretched the borders of the empire to the sea, nearly 200 miles (320 km) from Tenochtitlán.

Montezuma I and Tlacaélel continued the triple alliance with the states of Texcoco and Tlacopán, for mutual defense and profit and to capture prisoners for sacrifices. They agreed to share the prisoners and riches and lands they gained from the other tribes they conquered.

Besides his skill in war and politics, Montezuma I worked to help his people. With the aid of Nezahualcoyotl (ne-za-wal-KOY-otl), king of the Texcocans, an aqueduct was built to bring fresh water to the city from springs 3 miles (4.8 km) away in the forest of Chalpultepec. They also had a 12-mile (19.2-km) dike constructed, to control the flooding of the lake water during the rainy season. Under Montezuma I, Tenochtitlán grew to a fine city of stone, with impressive temples and sculptures and gardens—the heart of a rich and flourishing empire.

In 1469 Montezuma I died and Axayacatl (ash-ay-AH-katl) was chosen to succeed him. For the next ten years the Aztecs spread their control to the west and the south. Axayacatl led his warriors against the Tarascans, but was badly defeated. The Tarascans remained independent until the arrival of the conquistadores.

The Aztecs settled—as their god had ordered— where they saw an eagle perched on a cactus. This map, from the Codex Mendoza, *shows their island city of Tenochtitlán, set in Lake Texcoco. The founding ruler, Tenoch, is to the left of the cactus, with other nobles around him. Below the map, Aztec warriors topple the temples of rival cities. The border squares are glyphs for the Aztec calendar years.*

[13]

In this stone carving, the eagle—an important
Aztec symbol—is seen devouring a human heart.

In 1481, Axayacatl died of a wound he had received several years before, during a battle. His brother Tizoc, "Bloodstained Leg," succeeded him. Tizoc's reign ended in 1486 when he was poisoned by his own lords, who claimed he was a cowardly military leader.

Tizoc's brother Ahuitzotl (ah-WEET-sotl), "Water Dog," came to the throne and was a forceful ruler. The combined armies of the Aztecs and Texcocans swept down on the Mixtecs and the Zapotecs. The two-year campaign produced more than twenty thousand prisoners. They were brought back to Tenochtitlán and lined up in two rows. The two victorious kings began slashing open the captured victim's chests, snatching out their hearts, and offering them to the gods. The ceremony went on for days, and lesser lords in turn took over the grisly task.

Ahuitzotl sent his armies as far as the Pacific Ocean, south to Guatemala, and east to the Gulf of Mexico. In addition, his soldiers were constantly called upon to put down the revolts of previously conquered tribes.

In 1502 a flood broke the dam built by Nezahualcoyotl and Montezuma I. Some scholars think that Ahuitzotl died after being hit by a stone while overseeing repairs on the dam. He was succeeded by his nephew, Montezuma II, in 1503. This powerful ruler overran his former allies, the Texcocans, and captured many other city-states.

Under Montezuma II, the Aztecs controlled an empire that stretched to what is today Honduras and Nicaragua. But signs of weakness and strain were already appearing. The subject tribes resented the Aztecs' ever-growing demands for tribute and for victims for their ritual sacrifices, and their hatred for Aztec rule was increasing. For some years, too, the Aztecs had been troubled by strange signs and omens—fires, a comet, a small black speck that had been seen to cross the face of the sun, ghostly sounds of crying through the night in Tenochtitlán. Then alarming news was brought to Montezuma II, of white men in strange boats that had been seen along the Maya coast, near what is now Yucatán. Finally, in April, 1519, the Spanish conquistador Hernán Cortés—with a fleet of 11 ships, carrying 100 sailors, 508 soldiers, and 16 horses—reached the Gulf Coast near today's Veracruz, and began his march to Tenochtitlán.

[15]

3

THE AZTECS,
PEOPLE OF THE SUN

By the time the Spanish arrived in Mexico, the ambitious Aztec rulers had created a powerful state and a strong, tightly run society. Tenochtitlán ruled about eleven million people, and controlled the territory of nearly half of modern-day Mexico.

The Aztec people themselves—the hardworking farmer-warriors who were the strength of the empire—had moved far from their barbarian beginnings as a rough, wandering people with few skills.

The Aztecs were small by our standards. The women averaged about 4 feet 8 inches (142.2 cm), while the men were 5 feet 2 or 3 inches (157.5 or 160 cm) tall. Their complexions were a bronzelike brown; their eyes and hair were black. Both men and women wore their hair long. Because Aztec men, like other American Indians, had very little hair on their faces, shaving was uncommon.

In the Aztec society, there were sharp divisions between the social classes and strict rules governing each class. These rules covered many aspects of life, including what people of different classes could wear. The common people's clothes were made of fiber from the agave plant, while the higher classes could wear cotton. All Aztec men wore a *maxtli* (MASH-tlee), or loincloth. This was a long strip of cloth that was wrapped around the waist, passed between the legs and tied in front. They also wore a white cloak, or mantle, called a *tilmantli* (teel-MAN-tlee). A peasant's *tilmantli* could not reach below the knees and had to be tied over the right shoulder. An upper-class man could wear a longer cloak and could tie it under his chin. Since Tenochtitlán's climate was moderate, with warm, mostly sunny days and cool nights, the loincloth and cloak were the only clothing needed.

Aztec women wore an ankle-length skirt called a *cueitl* (KWAY-tl). This piece of cloth was wrapped around the body and held by an embroidered belt at the waist. A *huipilli* (wee-PEEL-lee), a long blouse with slits for the head and arms, was worn outside the skirt. Women often wore two or three skirts and blouses of different lengths, one over the other. They wore their hair long and straight or, when they worked in the fields, twined around their heads.

The everyday clothing of the common people was white, but for special occasions both men and women wore colorful embroidered clothing. On those special days, only, they wore sandals called *cactli* (KAK-tlee). These sandals were made of animal hides or agave fibers. They had heel pieces and were held on by crisscross straps.

Noble families dressed as the commoners did, except that their clothing was finer, of cotton, and beautifully embroidered in brilliant designs. Their sandals were sometimes made of jaguar skins or were painted turquoise or decorated with precious stones and gold.

Men and women of the nobility wore jewelry: necklaces, ear-plugs, and arm and ankle bracelets. The noblemen pierced their noses and wore jewels in them. They also made a hole beneath their lower lip and filled it with an ornament of gold, turquoise, shell, or crystal. Only the king could wear a turquoise ornament in his nose.

The nobles also wore cloaks and magnificent headdresses made of feathers. The most prized feathers were those from the rare quetzal bird, found in the Guatemalan highlands.

The houses of the common people had only one room, with a partition that separated the sleeping area from the living-eating area. The walls were built of reeds and mud. The roof was made of reeds and grasses, and the floor was packed earth. There were no windows and only one doorway. The higher classes and nobles lived in adobe—

sun-dried clay brick — or stone houses with many rooms and doors arranged around an inner court planted with flower and vegetable gardens. These houses were usually painted white.

The Aztecs' day began before dawn with the blowing of conch shells and the beating of great drums atop the temple-pyramids. Women rose and lit their house fires. Men went out to the *temascalli*, the steam bath close by their homes. The *temascalli* was a round little building of stone and cement. Outside one wall a fire was lighted, and when the stones were sufficiently hot, the bather crept into the building through a small low door and threw water on the inside of this wall. Soon the building was filled with steam, and the bather used long grasses as a scrub brush. Common people who did not have a *temascalli* bathed in a nearby canal or in the lake that nearly surrounded Tenochtitlán. The Aztecs did not have soap, but they did have two plants that produced soaplike substances, one from its fruit and the other from its roots.

In the morning the women boiled maize and then ground it in *metates* (me-TAH-tays) — hollowed-out slabs of stone. The *metate* held the maize while a kind of rolling pin called a *mano* was worked back and forth to crush the corn. The maize was then patted into large, round, flat cakes and cooked over the fire in a *comalli*, a flat clay cooking plate. These maize cakes, called *tortillas* (tor-TEE-yas) by the Spanish, were eaten every day.

The men usually left their homes at dawn, without breakfast. In Tenochtitlán they poled their dugouts along the canals to their fields or *chinampas*, the floating gardens. At about ten o'clock in the morning they drank a bowl of *atolli*, a corn gruel, or porridge, that was sometimes sweetened with honey or spiced with pimento. By midafternoon the famers returned for their main meal of the day. The men took their meals squatting on mats called *petatls* (pe-TAH-tls), which were placed around the hearth. Women and children ate separately from the men.

The Aztecs ate maize cakes, many kinds of beans, sweet potatoes, onions, peppers, avocados, tomatoes, squashes, fruits, fish, and on special occasions, meat. But meat was scarce, and the only kinds available to the common people were turkeys, and perhaps ducks, and small

[18]

hairless dogs that were raised for food. In the homes of the lords, however, a wide variety of meats was served: turkey, rabbit, deer, duck, pheasant, quail, partridge, wild boar, and the small dog. They also had such luxuries as vanilla, chocolate, tropical fruits of all kinds, and tobacco for smoking, imported from the hot lands near the coasts.

Because the Aztecs were lake people they ate things that were found in or near water: fish, frogs, freshwater shrimp, worms, snails, turtles, and snakes.

In the fading light of day and by firelight, men sharpened or mended their farming, hunting, and fishing tools. Women sewed, spun thread, weaved with a backstrap loom, and prepared corn for the next day. With the sound of conchs and great drums in the temples the day came to an end. Grass mats were unrolled and placed on a raised level of earth in the houses, and everyone went to bed. For, according to Sahagún, the Aztec day was marked by nine time divisions. The conchs and drums sounded at sunrise, midmorning, noon, sunset, the beginning of night, bedtime, the time for prayers by the priests, a time shortly after midnight, and rising time, a little before dawn.

The Aztec farmer needed to work his lands only 200 days out of the 365-day year to produce 200 bushels (7,050 l) of corn. This was more corn than his family needed, so he used the surplus to pay taxes or to barter for weapons, clothing, meat, or whatever caught his eye in the marketplace. But after two years—two crops—the soil was exhausted. A part of the *milpa*, the cornfield, would have to be left idle for ten years before it could be used again. Thus, the average family had about 10 acres (4 ha) of land, but only a small part was planted each year.

The land was not owned by the farmer. The land belonged to the calpulli (kal-PUL-lee). In the early days of the Aztecs a *calpulli* was a group or clan made up of related families. But at the height of the Aztec rule a *calpulli* became more like a political district.

All the land of the *calpulli* was divided by the *calpullec*, the chief of the calpulli. Each household was given a share to work. If a farmer—the head of the household unit—died, the land went back to the *calpulli*, to be shared out again. Usually the *calpullec* allowed the

[19]

farmer's family to keep the land and work it. A lazy farmer or one who produced poor crops lost his land.

To prepare a new *milpa* the Aztec farmers first cut down the trees with stone axes. The bush and trees were then burned, and the wood ashes were used to fertilize and loosen the soil. Later, at planting time, the famers used a *coa*, a digging stick, to turn over the earth and to make holes in the ground for the kernels of maize. Between the rows the farmers planted beans and squashes. Besides these and many other vegetables, the Aztecs also planted flowers.

One of the most important plants native to Mexico was the agave or maguey (ma-GAY). Its large, thick blades were used for roofing huts. After being beaten and dried, the blades yielded fibers for making clothing or rope. At the end of each blade is a spine like a needle. When this was bitten or cut in a certain way it would come free, bringing along its own fibers of thread, ready for sewing. The spines were also used, in rituals, to cut or slash the body.

Peeled maguey blades produced thin sheets of paper that could be used for writing. When the plant's center was cut out, a core or heart which contained sap was revealed. This was fermented to make a cidery-tasting beer called *octli* by the Indians. Drinking was frowned on in Aztec times, and normally only old people were allowed to drink. The punishments for public drunkenness ranged from having one's head shaved to being beaten or strangled to death. *Octli* was drunk by those who were not old, therefore, only on special family and religious occasions.

This huge sculpture of Coatlicue, the earth or mother goddess, was found beneath the central square of Mexico City. It had been buried when the Spanish destroyed the Aztec capital, Tenochtitlán. The goddess's head is formed by two rattlesnakes, and her skirt, too, is made of snakes. Around her neck is a chain of hearts and hands, ending in a skull. Her feet have claws like those of a jaguar.

[21]

The ruins of the ball court at Monte Albán
include rows of stone seats for spectators
lining the sides of the central playing area.

In addition to farming, the Aztecs hunted and fished. Birds were brought down with stone pellets from blowguns; small animals were caught in traps; fish were caught in nets thrown from dugouts. Only the nobles were allowed to hunt with bows and arrows for larger game such as deer, as these animals had almost all been killed off in the Valley of Mexico.

The work-filled routine of the Aztec families was often broken by religious festivals and rituals. The people also enjoyed occasional games. One popular dice game was called *patolli*. Players used a board shaped like a cross, divided into fifty-two squares. Beans marked with spots were the dice, and colored stones served as the players' markers on the board. The players took turns throwing the beans and then moving their markers for as many squares as had been shown on the beans. The winner was the player who returned "home" first.

Another game, *tlachtli* (TLATCH-tlee), was played only by the nobles, but it was watched by large crowds of people from all classes. There were two teams of players in a court shaped like the capital letter *I*. The teams faced each other in the long part of the *I* and tried to hit a 6-inch (15.2-cm) round, solid-rubber ball into the other team's part of the court. There was also a stone hoop in the center of each side wall of the court. If a player could pass the ball through one of the hoops, the game was over, and that team won. But this seldom happened, as the hoops were placed vertically, and the ball could be struck only with the trunks of their bodies and perhaps their elbows. The game was very rough, and the players wore heavy padding and leather gloves to protect themselves. The Aztecs loved to gamble on these games, and betting ran very high. Gold, slaves, clothing, even houses and land were won and lost. If a team put the ball through one of the hoops, the winning players and bettors could snatch the clothing from the backs of the losers.

These two games, *patolli* and *tlachtli*, had religious meaning. The cross-shaped board stood for the four directions of the gods, and the fifty-two squares for the fifty-two year sacred time period; the *tlachtli* ball court was the world and the rubber ball was a symbol of the sun. For the Aztecs, nearly everything had religious meaning.

[23]

4

TRAINING FOR
THE AZTEC WORLD

The Aztec family greeted the birth of a child with joy, and with many rituals. The midwife who delivered the baby performed the birth rites. She welcomed the child and warned of the dangers of life ahead. Family members and all the community came to greet the child and bring gifts. The priest was called to consult the *Tonalamatl* (to-NAH-la-MAH-tl), the "Book of Fate," to see if the birth day was lucky or unlucky. If it was lucky, the child was named at a family ceremony the next day. If it had an unlucky sign, the priest would see if any of the next few days had better omens, and the family could then put off the naming ceremony. The sign of the birth day was important throughout life. For example, a child born under the day-sign 1 *Ocelotl* (os-e-LO-tl) would die as a prisoner of war; but a child born on 1 *Calli* might become a fine doctor.

Children were given unusual, colorful names. A boy might be called Chimalpopoca, "Smoking Shield"; or Itzcóatl, "Obsidian Snake"; or Nezahualcoyotl, "Hungry Coyote." Or he might be named for his birth date, such as Ce Acatl, which means "One Reed." Girls often had names that ended with the word "flower," *xochitl*, such as Quiauhxochitl, "Rain Flower," or Matlalxochitl, "Green Flower."

[24]

At the age of three, the children's education began. Their parents lectured them on the importance of duty, hard work, and leading a good life. Pictures in the *Codex Mendoza* show that a three-year-old was given one-half a maize cake each day. Four- and five-year-olds were given one whole cake a day. From ages six to twelve, children received one and a half cakes. From thirteen on, they were given two maize cakes a day. They had many other things to eat—vegetables, fish, occasionally meat. But these food rules were part of the strict upbringing of all Aztec children.

From the ages of three to six, children did small household chores. If the children disobeyed, their punishment was harsh. They might be pricked with maguey needles, or left tied up in a mud puddle overnight. After the age of six, boys learned farming, fishing, or their father's trade; girls learned their mother's tasks—cooking, weaving, making clothes, child care.

In the Aztec world, every child went to school. We are not sure of the age at which they started: some scholars say between six and nine; others believe they began at twelve. There were two kinds of schools. Most children went to the clan's school, the *telpuchcalli* (TEL-pootch-KAHL-lee), or "house of youth."

The boys' *telpuchcalli* taught citizenship; religion and ritual dances, songs, and music; and history, crafts, and the use of weapons. Since most of the teachers were soldiers who had earned the right to teach by capturing prisoners in battle, the emphasis in the school was on the use of weapons and on war.

According to Sahagún, life at the *telpuchcalli* was hard. The boys were allowed to go home for meals and to learn their father's work, but they had to sleep at school and had many chores. They swept the temple steps, kept the sacred fires going, did farm work and building, and helped the priests. All the while they were learning the art of warfare. When the army went to war, the young students went too. They served under the warriors in battle.

In the evening, after school, according to Sahagún, they went home, bathed, painted their bodies, and went to the *cuicacalli* (KWEE-ka-KAHL-lee), the "house of song." There they sang and danced until midnight.

[25]

When a *telpuchcalli* student captured his first enemy warrior, he was allowed to cut off the braid he had worn on the back of his head up to that time. In addition, he could leave school. But a boy who failed to bring back a prisoner after several battles was considered a disgrace. He, too, could leave school, but would never be able to hold any office or wear fine clothes. Boys were also allowed to leave the *telpuchcalli* when they wished to marry and take up farming or a trade.

The girls' *telpuchcalli* were run by priestesses. The girls were taught the skills they would use in family life, and the healing arts, and religion and ritual music and dance. Discipline was as strict for them as for the boys.

The second kind of school was the *calmecac* (kahl-MAY-kahk), or temple school. These were attended mostly by the children of nobles, although the promising child of a poor family could also attend. The higher education offered in the *calmecac* prepared young men to become priests and chiefs or high officials.

If life was hard at the *telpuchcalli*, it was even harder at the *calmecac*. Besides all the duties required of the students at the *telpuchcalli*, *calmecac* students were taught manners, discipline, self-control, and self-denial. At night, for instance, they would rise and go into the mountains to burn incense to the gods. There they pricked their legs

These pictures from the Codex Mendoza *show the education of children from the age of three, at the top, to six, at the bottom. On the left, a father instructs his son; on the right, a mother instructs her daughter. At three, the children are given verbal instructions and half a maize cake at each meal. At four, the boy fetches water; the girl learns the contents of her workbasket, and they are each given a whole maize cake. At five, the boy carries light loads of wood or grass; the girl learns to use a spindle. At six, the boy is sent to the market; the girl learns to spin. They are given one and a half maize cakes at each meal.*

[27]

and ears with maguey spines and offered the blood to the gods. On other nights, they bathed in the freezing lake waters. They were expected to fast and do penance. Punishment for not greeting and speaking politely to others was severe. The school built strong character and stout bodies to face suffering and pain. The priests taught the young students history, the holy songs written in their books, reading and writing, astrology, counting time, and the interpretation of dreams. A *calmecac* student was expected to have all the knowledge known to the Aztecs, and to be brave in battle.

The girls' *calmecac* trained them to become priestesses or the wives of high-ranking officials. They were instructed in manners, religious ritual, fine weaving, and featherwork.

If a young man or woman wished to leave the *calmecac* or the *telpuchcalli* to marry or to begin farming, the family invited the school's masters to a feast. After the meal, the elders of the family gave a polished stone ax to the masters and asked them to release the young person. When the masters accepted the ax and left the house, the student was free of further schooling.

Before a marriage, as at a birth, priests studied the signs and omens under which the bride-to-be was born. These signs were compared with the young man's birth signs. Men usually married at about twenty, and women at about sixteen. The marriages were arranged by the young man's family, with the help of old women who acted as go-betweens with the bride's family. After many polite refusals, and much discussion, the marriage plan was settled. The priest was again called upon to set a day for the wedding, which had to take place under good signs.

The day before the marriage a huge feast was held at the bride's house. Then she bathed, and her legs and arms were decorated with red feathers. That evening her future husband's relatives led the wedding party through the streets to his house. The bride was often carried on the back of an old woman. There was singing, dancing, and gift-giving. The wedding party feasted on large quantities of food and drink. Inside the house, the bride and groom sat on mats before the hearth. After many speeches by the elders, the ends of the groom's cloak were tied to the girl's blouse as the symbol of their marriage.

5

THE LADDER OF SOCIETY

When the Aztecs first moved into the Valley of Mexico, they lived in simple communities, *calpullis*, with simple social structures. The chief of each community was the *calpullec*.

By the time the Spanish arrived, there had been great changes. The *calpullis* were still the basis of the society. They owned the land. The *calpullecs* shared out the land among the families of the *calpulli*. They also saw to the cultivation of the land and the payment of taxes and tribute. Work on public projects and military service were organized by *calpullis*. But in Tenochtitlán and the large, thickly settled area surrounding it, a complex state had grown up on top of the *calpullis*. There were many classes and layers of society. There were vast differences in wealth and power. There were complicated systems or chains of authority. A separate priest class had developed, which also had power.

At the very top of the state was the king, the *tlatoani* or speaker. Around this powerful figure were two privileged classes—the *pilli*, who may have been a hereditary class of nobles; and the *tecuhtli* (tay-κοο-tlee), the administrators of the state. The king, his four mighty warlords and advisors, and high ranking officials were the *tecuhtli*.

[29]

The *tecuhtli* lived in palaces built and maintained by the people. They used the produce from the lands worked by the common people and were often given goods and clothing by the king—from tribute paid to him. They appointed officials to help them fulfill their duties.

From birth, every Aztec boy was dedicated to become a warrior. Schooling at the *telpuchcalli* trained him to fight. The way to gain power, a position, and riches was to distinguish oneself in battle. When an Aztec warrior had killed or captured four of the enemy, he was given the title *tequiua* (tay-kee-oo-ah), which meant "one who has [a share of] tribute." Then he became a member of the nobility. Each time he distinguished himself in battle he received more honors, a more richly decorated uniform and the right to wear a feathered head-dress, a greater share of the wealth, and command of a larger group of warriors. Thus through bravery a commoner could become a noble. This merit system helped strengthen the Aztec people. It allowed able and ambitious men to gain power.

Below the nobles were the common people, the *macehualtin* (MAH-se-WAHL-teen). They had many obligations: they worked their lands, paid taxes, and served as warriors. They also were called on to clean, maintain, and build roads, canals, bridges, and temples, and for other public work. To balance this heavy load of duties, they had the rights of full citizens. They had the right to farm their plot of land and send their children to school. They took part in rituals and could vote for local chiefs. When clothes and food were given out by their rulers, they received a share. And they had the right to rise above their class—through good fortune or through their own efforts.

The warriors in this codex picture wear fine, colorful uniforms and carry decorated shields and obsidian-bladed war clubs.

79.

Below the *macehualtin* were the *tlalmaitl* (tlal-MAH-eetl), a class of tenant farmers. These people were not citizens and had no claim to land. They worked the fields of some noble and had to pay rent. They also acted as the noble's servants. The *tlalmaitl* did not pay taxes or work on public projects, but they served in the army.

At the bottom of Aztec society were the slaves. A slave, a *tlacotli* (tla-KO-tlee), was neither a citizen nor free. Slaves belonged to their masters. Strangely enough, slaves could have money and own things. They could have their own slaves, and they could even buy themselves out of slavery. They were not mistreated. They were fed, clothed, and housed as well as common citizens. A slave might marry—either another slave or a free person. Their children were born as free people.

During hard times, free citizens sometimes sold themselves into slavery for a certain period. After being paid something like twenty pieces of cloth, the slaves-to-be remained free until they had spent this pay, then began to serve.

Other slaves were prisoners taken in war, or were part of a tribute paid by a conquered territory. For some crimes, the punishment was slavery, and criminal slaves were the lowest group.

Lazy or thieving slaves were given three chances, under different masters, to mend their ways. If they failed to do so, they were sold as victims for sacrifice. If slaves escaped in the marketplace, only their own masters or their masters' sons could give chase. If they reached the king's palace before being caught, they were free.

Two special classes in Aztec society were the *pochteca*, the merchants, and the *tolteca*, or craftsworkers. The *pochteca* (potch-TAY-kah) were daring adventurers. They traveled many hundreds of miles from Tenochtitlán on trading trips—buying goods in one area, selling in another. They often traded in enemy lands, and so were useful spies for the Aztec state. They reported to the king on the strengths and weaknesses of other peoples.

The *pochteca* lived as a class separate from the rest of the people. Their homes were in a certain part of each city. They had their own special god—Yacatecuhtli (YA-kah-te-KOO-tlee), "Lord Who Guides"—their own judges, and their own banner when they went to war.

In the Toltec capital of Tula stand these
18-foot (5.45-m) high stone warriors—
once part of a great pyramid-temple.

By the time the Spanish arrived, the children of the merchant class could attend *calmecacs*, which were generally the schools of the nobility. But the merchants were very careful not to display their growing wealth and power in front of the jealous nobility. They hid behind simple clothing and humble airs, because the nobles scorned them as people who were seeking personal gain, and were not true warriors.

The merchants made sure they arrived home late at night, in secret, after their long, dangerous trading trips. They quietly unloaded their packs of cotton, cacao, rubber, jade, pottery, feathers, nuts, herbs, medicines, and chicle—the gum of the sapodilla tree, which is used for chewing gum—and stored them under the name of a relative or friend.

There were no pack animals in Mexico before the time of the Spanish, who brought their horses with them. Although Aztec wheeled toys have been found, the Indians did not use wheels for transport. Everything was carried on people's backs. The *pochteca* often used slaves to carry their goods.

Craftsworkers were called *tolteca* (tol-TAY-kah), for their crafts were said to have been developed by the Toltecs—the ancient master builders in the Valley of Mexico. The highly skilled *tolteca* worked in gold, silver, turquoise, amber, pearls, amethysts, shells, feathers, wood, and stone. Workers taught the craft to their children and, occasionally, the children of the nobility. Although the *tolteca* paid taxes, they were not called upon to work on public projects.

WAR AND RELIGION

The Aztecs believed that when the sun set in the evening, it began a nightlong struggle against the powers of darkness. For the sun to be reborn—that is, for it to rise again in the morning—it had to be fed human blood and hearts. If the sun were not given this precious food, darkness would take over the world forever. As the chosen people of Huitzilopochtli, the Aztecs had the special responsibility, and honor, of keeping the sun god alive with blood sacrifices.

Human victims for sacrifice were taken mostly on the field of battle. Thus one purpose of war was to gain prisoners—not to kill or plunder. The need for prisoners for sacrifice led the Aztecs and some of their neighbors to invent a kind of ceremonial war, a War of Flowers, *Xochiyaoyotl*. These were battles that were arranged for the purpose of taking prisoners. The time, place, and number of warriors were agreed on before the battle. In one War of Flowers with the Cholulans, the Aztecs, who had captured enough prisoners, sent a messenger to see if the Cholulans were satisfied. When the messenger returned with word that they were, both armies ended the struggle and took their prisoners home to their sacrificial altars.

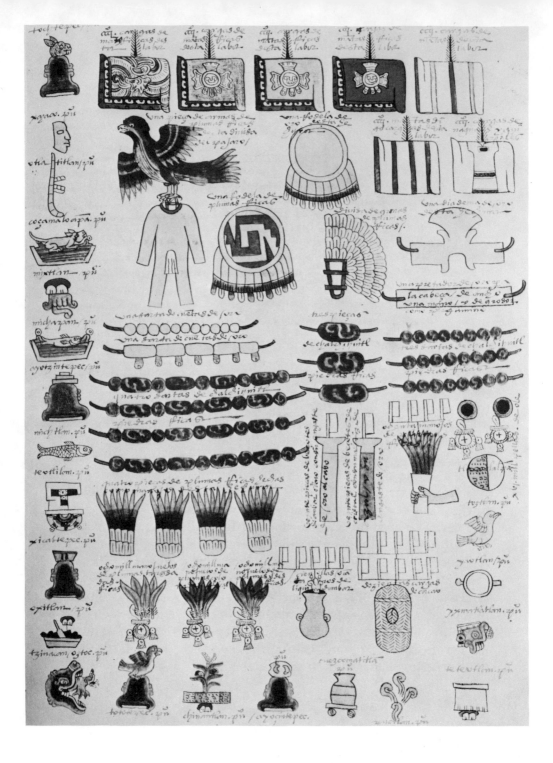

According to some Spanish writers, thousands of people were offered to the gods each year. During a terrible drought and famine in the mid-fifteenth century, the Aztecs sacrificed ten thousand victims. When the famine ended, the Aztecs were sure they had pleased the gods and continued the sacrifices.

But wars were not fought only for religious reasons. The Aztecs wanted to control the Valley of Mexico and claimed this was their right because they were the descendants of the Toltecs, the former rulers of the region. And, as Tenochtitlán grew to be the greatest power in the Valley, and its population increased, the Aztecs' need for more land, water, and goods became greater.

After the Aztecs had conquered new lands, they did not stay to rule them. The defeated peoples were allowed to keep their own leaders, but they had to pay tribute (in goods, foods, services, warriors, and slaves) to Tenochtitlán. The Aztecs did not build a true empire, ruled by one king and a central government. It was a loosely tied collection, or federation, of tribute-paying towns and cities.

To gain new subjects, the Aztecs often looked for an excuse to begin a war. If a *pochteca*, or merchant, was robbed, attacked, or badly treated while on a trading trip, the king and his council declared war. Since the merchants were used as spies, and were sometimes even told to cause trouble, it must have been hard for neighboring countries to prevent war from starting.

This illustrated tribute list from the Codex Mendoza *shows the payments a subject tribe had to make to their Aztec rulers: warrior suits, shields and headdresses, mantles, feathers, cotton, beads, and foods, including corn, beans, grain, honey, and peppers.*

[37]

Whatever the reasons for war—broken trade routes, political disagreements, or some incident—the Aztecs always tried to negotiate first. Politics were carried on in a formal manner. First ambassadors were sent with pleas and threats. If this failed, the ambassadors went again to see the enemy ruler, but this time they were rude. They covered the ruler's right arm and head with gum and feathers, placed a feathered headdress on his head, and presented him with weapons. Even after this insult, the ruler allowed them to leave the city alive.

The Aztec king then called in his advisors and the four great generals representing the quarters of the kingdom. Word was sent out, and a priest danced through the streets with a rattle and shield, announcing the war. Next the war drums sounded and the warriors assembled at the *tlacochcalco* (TLA-kotch-KAL-ko), "the house of darts," or arsenal, which was located next to the great temple.

The fighting men wore quilted cotton suits soaked in brine to make them stiff. These suits covered the whole body and were nearly as effective as a suit of armor. The great chiefs wore on their backs huge wooden frames decorated with brilliant feathers. Magnificent plumed headdresses, shields painted in a rainbow of colors, and feathered or multicolored cloaks were worn according to rank. The noblest warrior classes, the Eagle Knights and the Jaguar Knights, had special symbols. The Jaguar Knights wore the skins of the jaguar in battle, and the Eagle Knights wore helmets shaped like an eagle's head. Other helmets, made of reeds, bone, feathers, paper, cloth, and wood, were shaped and painted to resemble pumas or snakes.

A group of captains and their bravest warriors left the great square first. A day later the priests, with idols strapped to their backs, set out. On the third day the main army began its march in silence. Women went along to cook and to carry supplies. Because it was difficult to feed such a huge force, most battles lasted only a few days.

When the battleground was reached, the enemy ruler was called for a final conference. If this failed, a huge bonfire was lit, and incense was thrown into it. This was the signal of war. The warriors began whistling, howling, sounding drums and conch shells, and banging their weapons against their shields. In this deafening noise the first squads took to the field. They were archers armed with bows and arrows, and slingsmen who hurled stones from slings. Next came the lance or dart throwers. Lances were from 6 to 10 feet (1.8 to 3 m) long and were decorated with feathers and paper. The tips were of obsidian, a hard volcanic glass that was razor-sharp. Obsidian-tipped darts were hurled with great force by means of *atlatls* (aht-LAH-tls). An *atlatl* was a short wooden staff with a middle groove, and a peg at one end against which the dart fitted. When the *atlatl* was thrust forward quickly, it released the dart with great force.

Hand-to-hand fighters used sword-clubs called *maquahuitls* (MAH-kwa-WEE-tls), which had obsidian blades. The Spaniards found that these sword-clubs were so deadly they could cut off a horse's head in one blow. The Aztec shields were made of wooden wickerwork covered with animal hide. They were decorated with paint or feathers and usually bore the emblem of the warrior's clan.

The Aztecs depended more on numbers than on tactics or battle plans. When the main temple in the enemy's city had been taken, the war was ended. The victorious Aztecs then sent a runner to Tenochtitlán with his hair braided. He joyously waved a sword-club as he entered the city. But if the Aztecs lost, the runner entered the city silently, wearing his hair over his face.

Besides their duty to provide sacred food for the sun, much of the rest of Aztec life was also centered on service to the gods. For the Aztec world was full of mystery and fear.

The Aztecs saw the universe as divided into three worlds: earth, which was the home of human beings; the underworld, made up of nine separate layers; and the heavens, of which there were thirteen. Each heaven was different. In the fifth heaven, fire and fire snakes, comets, and stars wandered about. In the eighth heaven, obsidian-edged knives clashed and there were constant storms. Various gods lived in different levels of the heavens. In the highest heaven dwelt the original creators, the origin of all things, the Lord and the Lady, Ometecuhtli and Omeciuatl. They were the source of all the gods and of humanity.

After life on earth, a person's soul went either to a paradise or to the underworld, Mictlan (MEEK-tlan). Each soul's fate had been set by the sign under which it was born. Warriors who died in battle or were sacrificed to the sun, joined the sun in the heavens. Women who died in childbirth went to a western paradise. All those who had been chosen by Tlaloc, the god of rain, to die a watery death—by drowning or by lightning or certain diseases—went to the beautiful paradise of Tlalocan. Children who died early also had a special region in the heavens.

All other dead souls set out on a horror-filled four-year journey through Mictlan, the underworld. A small dog was their only company on the way. The souls had to avoid such dangers as two mountains that kept crashing together, wild beasts, deserts, and freezing winds that hurled obsidian knives. Finally, the traveling soul had to cross a wide river to reach the last, ninth underworld where ruled the lord and lady of the underworld, Mictlantecuhtli and Mictecaciuatl.

In addition to dividing the universe into layers—heavens, earth, and underworlds—the Aztecs also divided it into sections by the directions: north, south, east, and west. Each section was controlled by different gods.

The Aztecs had many gods, some scholars say over a thousand. Perhaps the greatest god was Huitzilopochtli, god of war and the sun. This was the stern hummingbird god, founder of the Aztecs, who had sent them in search of a homeland. Other important gods were Tezcatlipoca (tes-kaht-LEE-po-ka), "Smoking Mirror," who was god of the night sky; Quetzalcóatl (kayt-zahl-KO-atl), "Feathered Serpent," who was god of life and learning, and of the wind; Tlaloc, the principal rain god; his wife, Chalchiuhtlicue; Coatlicue (ko-at-LEE-kway), the earth or mother goddess; the maguey-plant goddess, Mayahuel; a corn god and goddess; gods of earth, death, water, sky, planets, stars, birds, animals, and more. Many of these gods had two-sided natures. That is, they could be good or evil.

An army of priests and priestesses was needed to serve these many deities, to interpret their moods and win their favor. The two highest priests lived in Tenochtitlán. Under them were priests who

[40]

*The sun god, Tonatiuh, appears at the left, and
the death god, Mictlantecuthli, is at the right
in this detailed drawing from the Codex Borbonicus.*

were in charge of the worship of each god. Other priests kept track of the tribute paid by subject peoples, and still others ran the priests' schools. Below these were thousands more who read signs, predicted future events, healed the sick, taught, and led the many ceremonies.

The main priestly duty, however, was conducting sacrifices. The victims who were to die on the altar wore fine clothing and were treated with respect, for they were representatives of the god to whom they were to be sacrificed. After a victim had been beheaded, or the heart was plucked out, priests smeared the blood on the idol of the god and on their own hair. According to Díaz del Castillo, the priests wore black robes and their hair was "very long and so matted that it could not be separated or disentangled . . . and it was clotted with blood." The priests stained their bodies black, and pricked their earlobes so often with maguey needles that they were shredded. Their lives were spent in fasting, praying, and burning incense.

7

THE AZTEC CALENDAR
AND OTHER
SCIENCES AND ARTS

The Aztec priests — besides serving the gods — had charge of all knowledge and learning. They taught time counting, picture writing, mathematics, astronomy, astrology, medicine, history, poetry, songs, and dance.

Like earlier people in the Valley, the Aztecs understood time and could measure its passing. They used two separate calendars. The sacred or ritual calendar was called the *tonalpohualli* (to-NAHL-po-WAHL-lee), or "count of days." There were twenty day names, such as crocodile, eagle, house. These were combined with the numbers from 1 to 13 to form a series of 260 days (20 x 13 = 260).

The second calendar marked the solar year. This calendar had eighteen months of twenty days each. As 18 x 20 = 360, the Aztecs added five "empty" or "unlucky" days to round out the solar year. Children born during the empty days were given names that meant "worthless" or "will never amount to anything."

It took fifty-two solar years for the two calendars to reach their starting points at the same time. The two calendars would then mesh. This fifty-two-year cycle was the sacred time period for the Aztecs.

The Aztec day-signs. 1. Crocodile. 2. Wind.
3. House. 4. Lizard. 5. Serpent. 6. Death's-head.
7. Deer. 8. Rabbit. 9. Water. 10. Dog.
11. Monkey. 12. Grass. 13. Reed.
14. Ocelot. 15. Eagle. 16. Vulture. 17. Motion.
18. Flint knife. 19. Rain. 20. Flower.

Every fifty-two years were bound or tied together, like a bundle of cornstalks, at a sacred ritual—the New Fire Ceremony.

The Aztecs feared that the end of the fifty-two-year period might mean the end of their world. So, on the last night of the cycle, they put out all their fires, smashed their pottery, and cleaned their houses. Many gathered on the hillsides to watch the heavens with the priests. When the stars finally gave the priests the sign that the world would continue, a fire was kindled on the slashed chest of the sacrificial victim. From this flame, sacred-fire torches were lit and runners sped across the countryside carrying the precious fire to the people—a signal that life would go on for another fifty-two years.

Each of the eighteen months in the solar calendar was marked with special religious celebrations. The first month, Atlcoualco (atl-ko-WAHL-ko), or "want of water," was celebrated with ceremonies, parades, and sacrifices. The celebration during the fourth month was in honor of the new corn. The eighth month brought the eight-day festival of eating ripened corn, and the sacrifice of a young girl who took the part of the corn goddess. Other months celebrated the gift of rain, the war gods, the fall of the fruits, and the return of the gods to earth.

The Aztecs had a written number system that they used for their calendars and in trade. A dot or a finger stood for the number 1. Dots were used for numbers up to 20. The sign of a flag meant 20. A single feather stood for 400, and a pouch or bag for 8,000. The Aztecs, like the Maya, used a "base twenty," or vigesimal, number system. We use the "base ten," or decimal, system.

The Aztecs also had a system for writing words. Hieroglyphs (glyphs) are pictures or symbols that stand for words. Many Aztec glyphs were simple pictures; bare footprints meant traveling; a burned temple pierced by a sword meant victory. Some symbols stood for certain sounds. Books, or codices, of these painted glyphs tell us much about the Aztec world. They describe wanderings, wars, kings, calendar counts, and travel events, and explain astronomy and astrology.

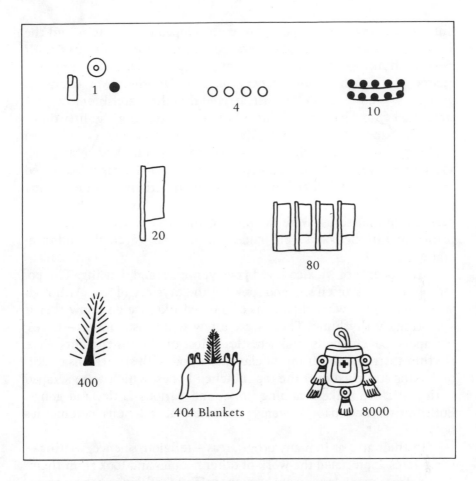

Left: the Stone of the Fifth Sun, often called the Aztec
Calendar Stone, shows the Aztec view of the world. The
face at the center is the sun god Tonatiuh. The four
squares around his face are symbols of the four earlier suns,
or eras, of the world. The next narrow band shows the
twenty day-signs of the Aztec calendar year. The outside
ring is formed by two fire serpents, their tails meeting
at the top and their heads at the bottom of the stone.
Above: the Aztec numbering system.

But this writing system had not been developed enough to record the amazing literature of the Aztecs: the beautiful poetry and stories, their moving hymns, prayers, and chants. This spoken literature was recited and taught to one generation after another over countless years. It was not until the Spanish arrived that the Aztec literature was translated from the Nahuatl language and written for the first time.

The paper used in Mixtec, Zapotec, and Aztec books came from the "paper tree," a wild fig tree. Sheets of the inner bark were stripped, soaked in water, and pounded with a stone. Later the paper was dried and coated with starch or lime, to make it smooth and white. A long strip was then folded over and over like a fan, and two thin boards, or perhaps animal skins, were fastened to the first and last pages. The paints used in the books were made from animal, vegetable, and mineral dyes.

The people of Mexico loved poetry, music, and dancing. The poetry was serious, often sad, and spoke of the mystery of life. Although we do not know what their music sounded like, we do know that it was strongly rhythmic. There were a few wind instruments—flutes, trumpets, conch shells, and whistles. Most of the instruments were rhythm instruments: drums of clay and wood with snakeskins or animal skins stretched over the top; notched bones, which were scraped with a stick to make a rasping noise; and various rattles and gongs. Both music and dances were performed at religious ceremonies only.

In their arts, as in many other areas—religion, science, writing—the Aztecs appreciated the work of other peoples and took from them. Artists from many lands were brought to Tenochtitlán, some by promises of wealth and position, some by force. There were Maya, Zapotec, Mixtec, Cholulan, descendants of the Olmec and the Toltec, and many other artists working with and teaching the Aztecs.

The artisans, or *tolteca* as the Aztecs called them, sculpted in stone, carved figures from rock crystal, turquoise and jade, painted murals and wall decorations, and worked in clay and, later, in gold and silver. To the Aztecs, jade was the most precious of all stones.

*One of the few Aztec buildings remaining is this
pyramid at Tenayuca. It was built over structures
of earlier peoples. Chains of stone serpents line
the base on three sides of the pyramid.*

The art of feather-working, brought to Tenochtitlán by the Mixtecs, was highly developed. They glued or wove magnificently colored
feathers onto a cloth backing to create feather-mosaic pictures. The
feather shields, cloaks, and headdresses were greatly prized. The
Aztecs also learned weaving and dying techniques from many peoples.
They used techniques of tie-dying, batik, embroidering, and many
others.

Besides being shaped into religious figures, clay was also used for
making everyday pots, bowls, cups, incense burners, dolls, and vases.
The people of Mexico at that time did not use a potter's wheel. The
pottery was formed by working coils of clay with the hands, and gradually building up the sides of the piece being made. By pasting on bits
of clay, or marking the piece with an obsidian knife, the artists created
lovely decorations. The pottery was often painted or decorated with a
variety of colors.

Almost no examples of Aztec architecture have been left for us to
study, because the Spaniards destroyed Tenochititlán. But from various Spanish reports, we know the city the Aztecs created was large and
impressive.

8

TENOCHTITLÁN, THE HEART OF THE AZTEC WORLD

On April 21, 1519, a force of conquistadores led by Hernán Cortés landed on the east coast of Mexico, at today's city of Veracruz. By November, Cortés and a band of his soldiers reached the great city of Tenochtitlán. On November 12, 1519, four days after entering the city, Cortés and his captains were invited to climb the 114 steps to the top of the great temple that stood in the great square of Tlatelolco. There Montezuma took Cortés by the hand, according to Díaz del Castillo, and "told him to look at his great city and all the other cities that were standing in the water, and the many other towns on the land around the lake. . . . So we stood looking about us, for that huge and cursed temple stood so high that from it one could see over everything very well, and we saw the three causeways which led into Mexico . . . and we saw the fresh water that comes from Chapultepec which supplies the city, and we saw the bridges on the three causeways . . . and we beheld on that great lake a great multitude of canoes, some coming with supplies of food and other returning loaded with cargoes of merchandise . . . and we saw that . . . it was impossible to pass from house to house, except by drawbridges which were made of wood or in canoes; and we saw in those cities Cues [temples] and oratories like towers and fortresses and all gleaming white, and it was a wonderful thing to behold."

Behind the Spaniards, on the pyramid's platform, stood twin shrines to the two great gods Huitzilopochtli and Tlaloc. They entered the shrine to Huitzilopochtli. Within the right-hand door stood the squat stone figure of the god, covered with precious stones, gold and pearls. About his waist was a belt of great snakes made of gold and precious stones. Around his neck hung a string of gold masks and silver hearts inlaid with turquoise. There were braziers holding burning incense, and the hearts of three sacrificed Indians. The walls and floors were black with the blood of many victims. According to Díaz del Castillo, the shrines smelled like slaughterhouses, and the battle-toughened Spaniards anxiously waited to leave.

On that day the Spaniards were looking at the greatest city in the Americas, a city of more than 250,000 people that covered more than 4.6 square miles (12 sq km). Below them in the great square was the marketplace, crowded with from 25,000 to 60,000 people. Díaz del Castillo wrote, "We were astounded at the number of people and the quantity of merchandise that it contained, and at the good order and control that was maintained, for we had never seen such a thing before."

The market in the great square at Tlatelolco was larger than that in the main square at Tenochtitlán. Both were conducted in the same way, however. Each kind of goods was always in the same place and in neat rows. Díaz del Castillo tells that gold, silver, precious stones, feathers, mantles, and embroidered goods were kept together. Next came the slaves who were for sale, some tied to poles, and some not. Then there were the traders in cloth and cotton. Cacao, or chocolate, was sold in another row. In other parts of the market there were row after row of fruits, vegetables, meats, pottery, sweets made of honey paste, paper, colors for dyeing cloth and for writing, herbs, oil-bearing seeds, salt, the skins of pumas and jaguars and foxes, knives of obsidian and flint, lumber, firewood, copper axes, rare flowers. "But why do I waste so many words in recounting what they sell in that great market?" wrote Díaz del Castillo, " — for I shall never finish if I tell it all in detail."

According to Cortés, stalls in the marketplace sold "medicines ready to be taken, ointments and poultices. There are barbershops, where one can be washed and trimmed; there are houses where, upon payment, one may eat and drink."

Soldiers policed the marketplaces. If an argument began, the opponents were taken to a court at one end of the area. Here three judges took turns in handing down on-the-spot verdicts. Stealing in the marketplace or along the highways was a serious crime, and the punishment was instant death by stoning. Other thieves were put into slavery until they had worked off the amount stolen or had paid back double what they had taken. Aztec laws were harsh, and punishment swift.

The center of Tenochtitlán was the great religious quarter. The "Wall of Serpents," decorated on the outside by figures of serpents, enclosed this vast area. Inside, the colossal twin pyramid-temple to Huitzilopochtli and Tlaloc dominated the square. At its center was the round temple to the great god Quetzalcóatl, god of life and learning, and of the wind. Its door was carved and painted to look like a serpent's mouth. Ball courts, raised altars, racks to hold skulls, and other temples filled this huge area. Beyond the "Wall of Serpents" was the beautiful palace of Montezuma. This huge building could be reached either on foot or by boat, for Tenochtitlán was truly an island city like Venice — a city of canals, lagoons, and fingers of water crossed by bridges and causeways.

According to Díaz del Castillo, "The great Montezuma was about forty years old, of good height and well proportioned, slender and spare of flesh. . . . He did not wear his hair long, but so just to cover his ears. His scanty black beard was well-shaped and thin. His face was somewhat long, but cheerful, and he had good eyes and showed in his appearance and manner often tenderness and when necessary, gravity. He was very neat and clean and bathed once every day."

His palace, with its many halls and luxurious rooms, was filled with people even at dawn, for this was when the Aztec day began. Government officials, singers, dancers, clowns, an army of servants, even artists and craftsworkers, all waited to be summoned — to consult with or to amuse their king.

[53]

Above: the Mexican scholar Ignacio Marquina worked from Spanish descriptions and from studies of Aztec ruins to develop this reconstruction of the sacred area of Tenochtitlán. The great temple where Cortés stood to survey the magnificent city is at the left. *Right:* the Codex Mendoza includes this drawing of Montezuma's palace. The ruler sits in his throne room at the top. Alongside are chambers where the ruler could meet his lords. Below are the military council room, to the left, and the civil council room, to the right.

Inside the palace walls were treasure rooms, kitchens, storage rooms, hanging gardens, a zoo containing jaguars and pumas, an aviary with rare birds, and lagoons edged with flower and herb gardens.

Other handsome palaces and public buildings stood beyond the walls of the religious center, facing on the great square. Like Montezuma's palace, their walls were colorfully painted and sculptured. Beyond the marketplace and great square were local temples and the white, one-storied houses of lesser officials, merchants, artisans, and the common people. These houses faced canals and footpaths, which were built side by side. The houses had no windows, but at the back of each was a court filled with flowers and vegetables.

Three raised causeways led from Tenochtitlán to the mainland. According to Cortés they were wide enough for eight horsemen to ride abreast. These roads also served as dikes: they were broken every so often by openings that were spanned by wooden bridges. These openings prevented the lake water from rising too high.

The rhythm of life for the Aztecs of Tenochtitlán was as regular and sure as the beat of the great snakeskin drum atop the Temple of Huitzilopochtli, which sounded nine times a day. The people poled their dugouts along the canals or padded barefoot along the earth-packed streets to work, to the markets, the temples, the schools, and the great public religious ceremonies.

Today Tenochtitlán lies buried about 30 feet (9 m) below Mexico City. The lake in which it once stood has dried up. The main square of the modern city lies almost on top of Tenochtitlán's great square. The palace of the president of the Republic of Mexico is built above Montezuma's palace. Whenever a new construction project is started in Mexico City, more treasures from Aztec times are uncovered. In 1978 diggers for a utility company found ruins of the great temple to Huitzilopochtli.

When the Spanish in 1519 marveled at the beauty of this temple, they did not realize it was a shell, and that it had been built over four or more earlier temples that had been erected on the same spot. The oldest, the first one built, was the work of the Aztecs who had settled Tenochtitlán. The rulers who followed put up larger and more magnificent temples, each ruler building over the earlier ones.

[56]

9

CORTÉS AND THE SPANISH CONQUISTADORES

Cortés and his small army had fought off thousands of Indians on their way from the Gulf Coast, over 200 miles (320 km) away. They had suffered from hunger, wounds, and exhaustion. With a force of four hundred Spaniards and about one thousand Indian allies, Cortés planned to conquer a nation that could easily put one hundred thousand warriors in the field.

Why did Montezuma allow the Spanish to approach his capital without a battle? Why did he even welcome them?

There are many reasons. The most important one is that Montezuma believed that Cortés might be the great god Quetzalcóatl, come to reclaim his people and lands. Quetzalcóatl was said to have left his country many years before, on a raft of intertwined snakes. The date of his departure was *ce acatl*. He promised to return on another *ce acatl*. The year 1519, the year the Spaniards arrived, was a *ce acatl* year, according to the Aztec calendar. Quetzalcóatl was thought to be white and bearded. Cortés was also white and bearded.

Another reason Montezuma was unable to act against the invaders was that the Aztecs had never seen horses, cannons, muskets, iron helmets, crossbows, or the huge mastiff dogs who fought by the side of

their Spanish masters. All these things were mysterious and frightening to the Indians.

Finally, the Aztecs had been having trouble for some time with several tribes near the Gulf Coast. These tribes deeply resented paying tribute and supplying sacrificial victims to Tenochtitlán. They welcomed the Spanish as liberators and became their allies.

Montezuma had tried to keep the Spanish from coming to Tenochtitlán. He had bribed them by sending ambassadors with rich gifts of gold, silver, jade, embroidered cloths, and a magnificent feather headdress. But the more the Spanish saw of these riches, the more they wanted Tenochtitlán.

An Indian woman, Malinalli, called Marina by the Spanish, played a large part in the downfall of the Aztecs. She had been given to Cortés as a slave and was devoted to him. She already understood both the Nahuatl and Maya languages and quickly learned Spanish. For her master, she worked cleverly on the frightened and superstitious Indians. There were as many plots and intrigues as battles between the Spanish and the Indian tribes. In time, the Spanish were able to get the powerful Totonacs and Tlaxcalans to join them as allies against the Aztecs.

Cortés and his small army entered Tenochtitlán on November 8, 1519. They were greeted by Montezuma and his nobles, and led to the old palace of Montezuma's dead father, on the great square. For a week, the Spanish spent their time admiring the splendid city, then Cortés made Montezuma his prisoner. For a few months the Spanish ruled the Aztecs through their king. Then Cortés had to leave Tenochtitlán for the Gulf Coast, to stop a rebellion led by one of his own countrymen.

This Aztec stone carving of the god Quetzalcoatl shows the god's head awakening in the feathered serpent's body.

[59]

While Cortés was away, his brutal lieutenant Pedro de Alvarado attacked a group of Aztecs who had gathered for a feast and killed them all. The people of Tenochtitlán rose in fury against the Spanish and forced them to take refuge inside the walls of the old palace. When Cortés returned, the Aztecs allowed him and his force to rejoin his troops inside. Montezuma tried to quiet his people, but he had lost their respect by allowing the Spanish to control him. His people stoned him and, a few days later, he died—according to Spanish reports. However, Aztec records say that he was murdered by the Spanish. Montezuma's brother, Cuitlahuac, became the new Aztec ruler.

The siege of the old palace continued until the Spanish, on June 30, 1520, tried to break out. But the noise of their early-morning attempt to escape the city attracted attention. An alarm was cried and the battle was on. Many of the Spanish tried to carry off Aztec treasures they had stolen and so—heavy with gold and jewels—they drowned while trying to swim the short distance to the mainland.

After allowing his surviving troops to rest, and getting a shipment of supplies, horses and men from Spanish Cuba, Cortés launched new attacks around the countryside. In December, 1520, the Texcocans swung over to the Spanish side. Their city gave the Spanish a base on Lake Texcoco and a chance to defeat the Aztecs. Cortés ordered ships to be built and armed with cannons. They would also carry musketeers and crossbowmen. As soon as they were afloat, they destroyed most of the Aztec war canoes on the lake. By June, 1521, the Spanish were free to invade the island city.

The Aztecs began to fight for their beloved sacred city, and their lives. Cortés soon realized that the only way to take Tenochtitlán was to destroy it gradually, filling in the canals with rubble to make roads for his horses, soldiers, and weapons. Each day more of their beautiful city was pulled down. Weakened by hunger and by outbreaks of measles and smallpox—diseases that were unknown before they were brought by the Spanish—the Aztecs gradually lost their strength and their will to resist. The ruler, Cuitlahuac, was among those who died. Finally, Cuauhtémoc (kwow-TAY-mok), the new king, tried to flee with his family in a canoe. They were picked up by one of Cortés's ships and taken to the Spanish leader. Cuauhtémoc was imprisoned and later put to death.

The Aztecs were worn down by the European method of warfare: prolonged battles, siege, destruction, and killing. They were used to short wars, with the purpose of capturing prisoners. The religion that had forged a mighty state contained the seeds of its destruction. Two worlds had clashed, neither understanding the other's warfare, worship, or way of life. The Aztec nation fell after nearly three months of constant fighting, on August 13, 1521.

FOR FURTHER READING

Blacker, Irwin R. *Cortés and the Aztec Conquest*. New York: American Heritage, 1965.

Glubok, Shirley, ed. *The Fall of the Aztecs*. New York: St. Martin's, 1965.

Karen, Ruth. *Feathered Serpent: The Rise and Fall of the Aztecs*. New York: Four Winds, 1977.

Stuart, Gene S. *The Mighty Aztecs*. Washington, D.C.: The National Geographic Society, 1981.

Vlahos, Olivia. *New World Beginnings: Indian Cultures in the Americas*. New York: Viking, 1970.

INDEX